Dung In My Foxhole

G.L. EWELL

Dung In My Foxhole

A Soldier's Account of the Iraq War, and his Post War Struggles with Injury and PTSD thru Poetry

Gordon L EweLL

Order this book online at www.trafford.com
or email orders@trafford.com

Most Trafford titles are also available at major online book retailers.

Printed in the United States of America.

ISBN: 978-1-4269-7058-0 (sc)
ISBN: 978-1-4269-7057-3 (hc)
ISBN: 978-1-4269-7094-8 (e)

Library of Congress Control Number: 2011908688

Trafford rev. 05/26/2011

 www.trafford.com

North America & International
toll-free: 1 888 232 4444 (USA & Canada)
phone: 250 383 6864 ♦ fax: 812 355 4082

To My Angel Alexandra, and her Arnold

She made my dream a reality

He defended my freedom in WWII, to chase it

"The Soldier above all other people, prays for peace, for he must suffer and bear the deepest wounds and scars of war."
-*General Douglas MacArthur*

PREFACE

The toughest of men, the "badest of the bad," those
who fear nothing more than defeat, achieve their
victories in part because they do not forget their
Creator, and seek his presence as they do battle, to
free the oppressed, and for the good of humanity.
                                                    -Gordon Ewell

How would you describe the magnificent array of colors in a brilliant
sunset, to one who has never had sight? How to relate the sweet
taste of sugar to one that has never tasted it? Could you explain the
beautiful smell of a rose to someone who could not smell?

How then does a Soldier let go of, or explain rather, the trauma
experienced in war to someone who has never seen, tasted, or
smelled the trauma of an intense meeting with the enemy? How
does a soldier begin to explain the traumatic sight of an enemy bullet
piercing the face of his "Battle Buddy," and blowing the back of his
head off? Or the deal with the trauma of witnessing an Improvised
Explosive Device (IED) detonating and blowing a "brothers" legs
off? How to explain the taste of blood, sweat, sand and tears mixed
together as they have streaked down your face and are tasted on
cracked lips? Is it possible to relate the smell of gunpowder escaping
a weapon as it ejects hot, spent rounds of brass; or the smell of
explosive ordinance, as mortar shells, or rockets explode nearby?
How about the smell of burning hair after a fireball has rolled over a
vehicle one is inside of; or the smell of an abdominal wound, as one
feverishly tries to save the life of a comrade; or the smell of death?

Any one of these events alone is traumatizing as a single event. Now imagine them all rolled together collectively as one single experience! One single intense fire-fight! Imagine a year of experiencing not just one, but many of these experiences. Imagine knowing every single day it was a possibility... every single day!

How does a Soldier, burdened with so many traumatic experiences, so many traumatic memories, so many nightmares, begin to pick and choose which one to try to share with someone first. Whether a counselor, family member or friend, how would you choose which experience to share first, to get someone to try to begin to understand all the feelings and emotions that go along with all the traumatic experiences. So many Soldiers keep them bottled up inside, solely because they do not know how to let them out, or are simply trying to protect others from exposure to the Hell that these memories and experiences have created, burned into, and scarred upon their mind... in my mind.

An unknown Civil War Soldier said "War is sheer boredom, interjected with moments of sheer terror." I totally agree. It is the moments of "sheer terror," that are so difficult for soldiers to let go of. The moments of "sheer terror," later became termed as being "Shell Shocked." Today it is medically referred to as Post- Traumatic Stress Disorder or commonly PTSD.

It is these moments, these memories that can be so hard for Soldiers to let go of. It is reliving these traumatic experiences that can become such a disability for the soldier. It could be, that the Soldier who is suffering from Post-Traumatic Stress Disorder (PTSD) would like to let go of their disabling experiences and haunting memories. It could also be, that the reason so many Soldiers suffer from PTSD, may simply be, like trying to describe that brilliant sunset to someone who has never had sight... these Soldiers may simply not know how to explain what they have seen and experienced.

In 2006 I was in the United States Army serving in Iraq. I was assigned to the Explosive Hazard Coordination Cell (EHCC), in the Route Clearance Section. My assignment was simple. I was to be embedded with each of the 39 teams in Iraq that had the mission of Route Clearance, or Bomb Hunting, and ensure that everyone was aware of the best Tactics, Techniques, and Procedures to use, especially with the new equipment being specially designed to aid the "Bomb Hunters." I was also to ensure these teams, were up to date on the current Tactics the enemy was using to make and disguise the bombs. I was simply, a vehicle, or rather a means, of rapidly gathering and sharing information.

The IED had become the enemy's weapon of choice, because of its devastating effects. In 2006, there were over 3,100 IEDs, or "Roadside Bombs," being found, or finding our Soldiers, every month. Over 100 roadside bomb "incidents" every day! Some of them found me. I was in a vehicle that was blown up by a roadside bomb on six different occasions. Mortar rounds have landed, and exploded next to my vehicle. The roadside bombs are often simply part of an enemy ambush. Once your vehicle is disabled, that is just the beginning of an event. What follows is often an attack on the disabled vehicle and those accompanying it, with everything from small arms firing (like pistols, rifles, and machine guns), to Rocket Propelled Grenades (RPGs), Rockets, and Mortars. During this time, I was severely injured. One time a bomb blew impacted wisdom teeth right out of my jaw, I suffered a broken neck, lost my hearing, lost an eye and most of the sight in my other eye, and suffered a Traumatic Brain Injury.

I was diagnosed with PTSD. This little book, stared out simply as a way for me to attempt to deal with my personal demons and nightmares associated with my own experiences from the War in Iraq. Not knowing how to let go of feelings, thoughts and experiences with others, I started to just place thoughts and memories as they would come, down on paper. After a while, I started to try and organize them a bit. At least I thought I could transfer them from "sticky notes," the back of envelopes, restaurant napkins, and gum wrappers onto the pages of a single note book. The more I wrote things down, the easier it became to deal with some of my personal demons. What has become of my scribbling was the idea for a book… this book.

I have assembled some simple poems, some written before I went to War, some while I was there, and some when I returned home, severely injured. I have also included a section of totally random thoughts that I refer to as "Gordy-isims" (my nickname is "Gordy"). I thought if the book was able to help just one person suffering from Post-Traumatic Stress Disorder (PTSD) to be able to try to share and "release" their own demons, it will have been worth it. If my little book is able to help anyone understand what someone suffering from PTSD is going thru, it will have been worth it. If it is able to help a counselor, or "Peer Facilitator" to help reach out to someone suffering from PTSD, it will have been worth it. For me, the experience of putting this book together and confronting some of my "own demons" has been "worth it." I hope reading my book will feel "worth it," to you as well! Thank you for supporting our Soldiers and Veterans, even if you disagree with war.

CONTENTS

Section One

The Poems

(Post War)

May 01st, 2011 [Bin Laden] 1

Angels Among Us...5

The Volunteer 9

Upon the Stairs 11

Inside My Head.. 13

Lonely 15

Not Together Anymore.. 19

Random Thoughts 21

"Demons" 23

Unspoken Bond 25

My Holiday Season 31

My Independence Day 33

Thank A Soldier Today.. 35

Recovery Road 37

I Want to Scream 41

All Over Again 43

"Stateside" 45

(Composed at War in Iraq)

My Last Mission...51

While Looking Out My Window...............................57

One Day Closer 59

Red, White and Blue..61

Again...65

"Barking" 67

Bombs..71

The End of My Day...75

Combat Engineer 77

(Pre-War)

Kiss Upon the Wind..83

Breath of Life 84

Star Filled Sky 85

Eternal Love 86

Your G.I. Joe 87

Apple Tree Love..88

Bus Window 89

Section Two
"Gordy-Isms"

(Random thoughts, comments and quotes collected from the "Post War" mind of the recovering Author. Each of them is original to the Author.)

List of Illustrations

Illustrated by Gordon L Ewell

The following illustrations are listed in the order in which they appear in the book. Listed first is the name of the illustration, followed by the poem or section it is associated with in the book:

01) Angel Wings (Angels Among Us, Not Together Anymore)

02) Volunteer Hands (The Volunteer)

03) Shadow People (Lonely)

04) Bonding Hands (Unspoken Bond)

05) Mistletoe (My Holiday Season)

06) Battle Cross (From Iraq Section Page)

07) Engineer Castle (Frontispiece and throughout "Poems from Iraq")

08) Glass Half Full (Beginning of "Gordy-isms")

May 01ˢᵗ, 2011 [Bin Laden]

Tonight the news story broke
On television our President spoke
America heard before going to bed
It was confirmed that Osama Bin Laden was dead

The man behind the attack on American soil
That made us all mad and made our blood boil
The man who's plan caused thousands to die
When hijacked planes became missiles in our skies
And smashed into the Twin Towers before our eyes

We rallied together as a nation and swore revenge
For loved ones lost both family and friends
We declared war and no matter the cost
Swore we would find Bin Laden and his terrorists
Even if we had to look under every single rock
And vowed to turn terrorist training compounds
Into giant parking lots

There would be no safe haven upon the globe
For anyone who wore the cloak of a terrorist robe

Bin Laden was pure evil no doubt
His dirty deeds would cause a holy man to shout
The whole world wanted an "Eye for an Eye"
And looked to America to carry that mission out
It took ten years for justice, but we got our "Eye"

May 01ˢᵗ, 2011 [Bin Laden] (Cont.)

We buried his body out to sea
So any loyal supporters had no grave to rally around
On the date of his death's anniversary
That news was very gratifying to me

Yes I am happy that Bin Laden died
For him I hope not a single soul cried
As for me my heart wept and I shed some tears
For fellow Soldiers who gave their lives
While fighting terrorists for these last ten years

For Wounded Warriors like me
His death did not take away our injuries
I am still deaf and missing my eye
And have a Traumatic Brain Injury, my TBI
Soldiers so severely wounded in this long fight

We cut the head off the monster no doubt
But we can't be deceived there are still monsters out
They will always be trying to plot an attack
We can't let our guard down we cannot turn our back
Or it will happen again and that is a somber fact

I am thankful for the news I heard tonight
But it won't take away my nightmares
When I turn out my lights
For myself and so many others
PTSD from this war will be a lifetime fight

<u>May 01st, 2011 [Bin Laden] (Cont.)</u>

That we fulfilled our promise to take Bin Laden out
Closed a chapter in "our book" for the world to see
And will forever be remembered in World History
As a great blow to Evil and Tyranny

And a reminder to Evil wherever it hides
"You mess with the Eagle or the justice it provides
The Eagle WILL find you, and peck out your Eyes"

G.L. EWELL

"Believe in them"

Angels Among Us

Angels are among us,
at each and every door

They walk beside us silently on city sidewalks,
out in the country and on sea shores

They walk beside us day and night
Ever ready to protect us,
if they are called upon to fight

Our Guardian Angels are there to help us,
to do things that are right

They help lift up our spirits and give us strength,
to battle with all our might

Life's battles come in many forms,
most are not physical you see

Most are mental judgments and decisions,
we must often make instantly

As we do our best to be good people,
and strive for that each day

Angels Among Us (Cont.)

Angels are always available to pick us up,
if we should stumble along the way

Yes Angels are here to help us,
each and every day

To contact them is easy,
all one has to do is pray

There are so very many ways,
that someone can pray

Not every single prayer,
is born from a bended knee

Some are kind and loving thoughts,
we think in reverence quietly

A thing they have in common,
each one from start

They are born from a desire for help,
or to "give thanks" from within our heart

Angels Among Us (Cont.)

Yes Angels walk among us,
and beside us it is true

Whether you believe in them or not,
I know that there is one watching over you

GLEWELL

G.L. EWELL

The Volunteer

One word has a special meaning
it is so vast and dear

It is truly known by those who it describes
the word is Volunteer

The Volunteer is a "Special Breed"

They perform miracles each day

They love the work they do indeed

And would not think of getting paid

Some say that they will be extinct
not in abundance anymore

I say they are still where help is needed
and often not asked for

They do their work for others
not seeking attention or accolades galore

They do their work with piece of mind and pride
and are seeking nothing more

They perform their deeds with reverence
and humility from the start

Simply giving "selfless service"
from their volunteering heart

<u>The Volunteer (Cont.)</u>

While far from becoming extinct

There will always be a need

For a special giving Volunteer
to perform a special deed

For until everyone gives a little of themselves
there will always be a place to stand

For a loving Volunteer
to lend a helping hand

G.L. Ewell

Upon the Stairs

I met a man upon the stairs
But when I looked, he wasn't there
He wasn't there again today
Oh how I wish he'd go away

He follows me from room to room
I've no place to roam that is not his own

I yell at him
Words he can't hear
Words that won't hurt him
He won't shed a tear

This makes me angry, I yell some more
I wish than man would find the door
Get the hell out of here
Bother me no more

Yet in my heart I know he's here to stay
You see this man can't go away

<u>Upon the Stairs (Cont.)</u>

This man couldn't leave
If leave he tried
Knowing this tears me up inside
God knows I have no place to hide

No place to run to escape his prying eyes
I am exhausted
Too tired now to care or even cry
Yes it tears me up inside

I met a man upon the stairs
Oh how I wish he wasn't there
He wasn't there again today
Oh God I wish he would go away

Inside My Head

There's a bomb inside my head
Time fuse is burning to the "det" chord up ahead

Why don't I hurry and "render it safe"
Why do I sit here, just watching, and wait

I don't want it to detonate
Yet still I do not move from my "frozen state"

Why don't I run, before it's too late
And get to that bomb, and "render it safe"

Why am I standing here, content to just wait

Is it because I have no family at home
Is it because I am tired of being alone

Is it because I am ready to move on
To leave it all behind, and dance to a new song

And be free of the pain, this horrible pain
I can feel with each breath, in my heart and my brain

Inside My Head (Cont.)

You cannot do that Soldier… It would be so wrong
While others believe, they have you to count on

So get up, get moving, it is time to act
You know what to do… what you're good at

There is a bomb inside of my head
That I must take care of, before I am dead

<u>Lonely</u>

Lonely is not a place to be
It is worse than Hell, or is for me

I long to be on a beach
Near the ocean or sea

But not alone, not just with me

I would like to travel on a train
But not alone, that would cause more pain

A Baseball game, NASCAR race, or Broadway play
I would like to see
So Many paces to travel, to wander, to be…

But not alone, not just with me

A town hall meeting, a county fair, any where
with a lot of people there

But I would still be all alone, and that to me
just doesn't seem fair

<u>Lonely (Cont.)</u>

Lonely is no place to be

But who would want to share life, with a
severely wounded Warrior like me

No matter how grand the house I roam
All by myself, it will never be a home

Lonely is no place to be
It is worse than HELL… or is for me

I need to get out of this place that I am in
Not out of my house, rather out of my skin

I need to unchain my brain
Before it finds me a grave

A friend, a crisis hotline
I doubt I would call

But I must do something
before I can't get up from a fall

I remember the story
"Footprints in the sand"

He was with me on missions
In that damn foreign land

I don't need a phone to make this call
I just need to take a knee; that is all

Lonely (Cont.)

And open up my heart
So his love can pour in

If I will just start
He will take over and do his promised part

Lonely is no place to be
And no one ever is
If they just remember their "knees"

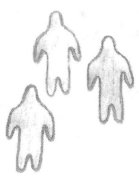

G. L. EWELL

GLEWELL

<u>Not Together Anymore</u>

I sit here with all alone
All these memories inside my head

Memories of a happy family that no longer is
That family now is dead

No, it is not each single member
That is dead

It is just the family unit,
That is not together anymore

The family unit it has been torn apart,
Ripped from its very core

It's the family now which is apart
That does not exist here anymore

My family, you see, it dissolved fast
When I returned home, with severe injuries from war

I had too many injuries
I had too intense of needs

With a severe brain injury
Even I did not recognize me

Slow to think and slow to speak
And often could not walk on my own

I could not eat or even sleep
I could not even answer a phone

<u>Not Together Anymore (Cont.)</u>

I could not see or even hear
It was confusing and filled me full of fear

I was intense to be near
And often hurt feelings of those I loved so dear

Everyone needed some time of their own
So my family found another home

Now I wander mine alone
And it hurts deep in my heart

I hope one day old wounds will heal
That perhaps there will be a fresh new start

And my family will move back home

Random Thoughts

Random thoughts race through my head
Random memories of War, of friends now dead

They bounce off the walls inside my brain
It is no wonder why I am in so damn much pain

What do I do now
How do I mend

How do I turn off the screams, inside my head
And replace them with happy memories instead

First I'll have to make some room, and let some go
But I am not ready to, they are ALL I know

They are sick and twisted, and hurt so bad
Why can't I let them go, to no longer be sad

I guess because they are a part of me
That I do not want to let go, just want to let be

I want to take them everywhere
But not to show, these memories I cannot share

<u>Random Thoughts (Cont.)</u>

Not because I don't love you
Or think you don't care

It is just that I am scared
You won't understand

What HAD to happen
In that God Damned Land

"**Demons**"

My demons come, and then they go
Where they go, I do not know

I know the date that they begun
It makes me mad, when at night they come

I know they will stay, 'til the morning sun
It makes my nights long and not much fun

It is at night they want to play
That is why I sleep at day

If sleep at all, will come my way
It is very rare, even during the day

I know they will be out again tonight
So again I prepare for another fight

My battle won't be won
With a knife or with a gun

I can only fight back with head and heart
So with my pen I have to start

To write things down, to make them run
Back to the HELL, that they came from

"Demons" (Cont.)

It is a battle that must be won
Fighting it sure won't be fun

I cannot continue to dodge the night
I must close my eyes and sleep to win this fight

It surly will be mighty hard
To face my demons in their own "backyard"

The nightmares I must let them come
If I want to see my demons on the run

When they come into my head
I'll write them on a pad kept by my bed

Yes, I will write them down and make them run
Back to the HELL that they came from

Unspoken Bond

Some things go without saying

They simply do not need to be said

One is a bond so strong

You never question it in your head

Such a bond is very rare

Once established it never breaks

It forever stays intact with you

Right up to your own death bed

There is no force of nature

No weapon strong enough to dent

No courtroom litigation that can break it or undo

This bond is not written or made with spoken breath

The special bond that exists between a special few

Is the bond of Combat Soldiers, willing to fight for you

Willing to protect our freedom and make it possible for

Other enslaved people to have a taste of freedom too

<u>Unspoken Bond (Cont.)</u>

Soldiers at War share this unique bond

Understood by very few

It is at its strongest at the very core

A foundation that starts with two

Each Soldier has a "Battle Buddy"

The bond starts with these two

They look out for one another

In everything they do

They train, eat, sleep and fight together

They know each other through and through

They build an unbreakable trust

A bond so strong no words are necessary

To say "I would do anything to protect you"

My "Battle Buddy" is the greatest

That any Soldier could ever have

No matter the circumstance I knew

Unspoken Bond (Cont.)

He always "had my back"

I would throw myself on a grenade for him

He would "take a bullet" for me and more

We never spoke about it out loud to each other

It was just understood and I felt it in my very core

 My "Battle Buddy" would give his life for me

And I for he, "The Unspoken Bond of War"

We spent over a year In Hell together

Everyday Death could "knock at your door"

In War there are NO guarantees

Except for that "Unspoken Bond of Brothers"

That lets you know for sure

That if Death came around knocking

There would be TWO to meet him at the door

I have not seen my "Battle Buddy" for some time

As I was severely injured while at War

<u>Unspoken Bond (Cont.)</u>

I was Medically Retired from the Army

He still wears the uniform, but one thing is for sure

Our bond it still remains intact, still at our very core

The "Unspoken Bond" of Combat Soldiers

That "Unspoken Bond of War"

"Peace-Out"

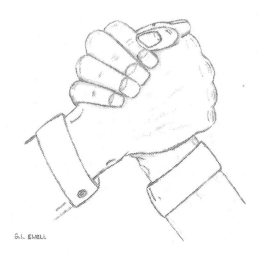

G.L. EWELL

My "Battle Buddy" and a Damn Good Soldier
SFC Kam Wright

Just outside Baghdad, Iraq (2006)

Statue of John Henry at the Maneuver Support Center in
Ft Leonard Wood, Mo (OCT 05, Prior to Iraq)

G.L. EWELL

<u>My Holiday Season</u>

Once again Christmas is almost here
A time to be merry and full of good cheer
The true meaning of "The Day"
Has long since gone away
Replaced by large debts from store "Layaways"

It should be a time for family to be near
Instead come excuses of bad weather to travel
And Vacation time gone, Used earlier in the year

I'm fine without crowds to be around
My PTSD would just have me trying to hide
All the noise and confusion is overwhelming to my TBI
It makes my head pound, so I try to escape
Somewhere warm and inside

Don't get me wrong, don't feel sorry for me
I'm not really complaining, just reflecting you see
Emotionally numb, I may not shed a tear
I wish you would not either; enjoy the carols you hear

Though broken and lonely, I am not distraught
Even though my mind drifts back to Battles I've fought
I do not feel slighted or cheated you know
I've battled in Rain, in Sand Storms, and Snow

I've battled and labored, fought hard, done my part
I have helped to protect Freedoms, so dear to my heart
Now I must forge ahead, and make a new start

<u>My Holiday Season (Cont.)</u>

What lies ahead, I don't know, I can't say
I'm sure there will be nightmares I just can't keep away
But for the most part, I will remind myself I am blessed
For I answered Lady Liberty's call, and
passed that part of life's test

For everyone else, I wish the best of this Holiday
Myself I will wish to just get through the day

I look forward to starting fresh come New Year's Eve
Pursuing new goals I would like to achieve
Like helping others like me, seek a new "Inner Peace"
That I know we can have; this I truly believe

I must move forward, be proactive and start
To find peace of Mind, of Body, and Heart

G.L. EWELL

My Independence Day

My Battles are over
But my war is not through
My body still has a lot of healing to do

I try to pick-up the pieces
And put them together each day
But then night comes along and
PTSD, Depression, and Anger blow all the pieces away

For a Combat Veteran, some wars never end
And try as they might, the memories still creep in
Memories of Family and loved ones
They thought of each day
Memories of Fallen Comrades lost along the way
And of hometowns they longed for, while hearing a
Chaplin pray

When wounded, a Purple Heart they place
Upon your chest
It is a beautiful medal, but it doesn't give all
Those memories a rest
When a soldier returns home, the memories don't hide
Too often they come out through drug use
Abuse and suicide

So here it is, Independence Day, with celebrations
Throughout the day
Some soldiers wish they could just hide somewhere
Quiet and out of the way
It's not easy to "Eat Drink and Be Merry," with bad
Memories in the way

<u>My Independence Day (Cont.)</u>

If you see a Soldier or Veteran, I wish you would say
"Thank-you for serving, and preserving freedoms
Like this holiday"

You may hear a sniffle, or see a wet eye
But that is part of the healing
Dealing with demons inside

"Thank-you," so easy to say
But to a Soldier or Veteran, that "Thank-you"
Will go a mighty long way

<u>Thank A Soldier Today</u>

The war is not over
The job is not done
But where is America
It seems her citizens have run

Yet each day the Nation's Soldiers fight
They fight terrorists by day and by night
And each day some are wounded
Each day we lose some

For these Soldiers and their families
The war is still real
Even though for television news
It has lost its appeal

For the severely wounded the war may never be done
Their road to recovery will be a long one
And the nightmares, Lord knows
They will all have some

But ask anyone if they would
Trade in their "lot"
No, not a single one
For their Honor and sacrifices for freedom
cannot be bought

Thank A Soldier Today (Cont.)

So I say to our citizens
Pull your head out of the sand

Rally behind those fighting
For this country's values and land

And don't let politics blind you I say
Like the saying goes "forget the war not the warrior"

Thank a Soldier or a Veteran today
That "thank-you" will go a mighty long way

Recovery Road

So, you have found yourself here in wing 7D
It's not at all where you would choose to be
You would not pick to have a Traumatic Brain Injury
And you would not have chosen to also have PTSD

You are missing an arm or a leg
Maybe a double amputee
Your thoughts are all garbled, and random as can be
In a split second your mood changes, to
Bitter and then to angry

And again, with no warning at all, it shifts to a teary
Depressed bundle of "Why me?" and self-pity
I know how it is, I know how you feel
For you see, **I have been in your shoes**, In wing 7D

Right now you might not think
A "happy ending" could possibly
Come out of what happened to you overseas
But that ending is out there my friend; you must have Faith and
believe

We rally around each other, quite literally
For Hope and Support and the Love that we need
It won't make the "Recovery Road" pain-free, trust me
It **will** make it easier to travel, hang in there, you'll see

Don't ever give up, ever quit, ever "Cower"
And don't be afraid to cry, those tears give you power
Trust in your providers, most I know personally
They truly care about you, just as they cared about me
Some more friends of mine will be there regularly

<u>Recovery Road (Cont.)</u>

They are the "Blue Star Riders," and they
Are awesome —you'll see
They want to help boost your morale, and they
Sure did it for me

You will ***NEVER*** be the same old you
That guy is gone
Save yourself some misery, quit looking for him
It's time to move on

But soon a "new you," you will be-friend
And if you want it, a happy and productive life
You can enjoy to the end

Some of my "Recovery Road" photos

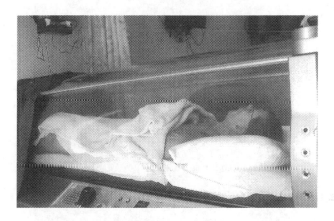

Hyperbaric Oxygen Chamber Treatments for my Traumatic Brain Injury.

This is my first look at my one eye; with "one eye."

Some of my "Recovery Road" photos (Continued)

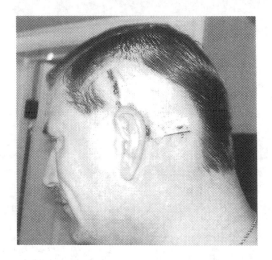

After the surgery to insert a Cochlear Implant.

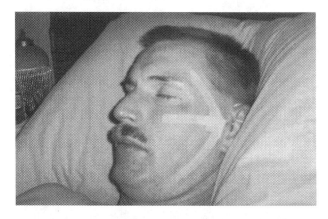

Recovering from a surgery to repair torn ligaments, replace cartilage with cheek muscle and "build up" of the mandible ball joint and cheek bone to later attach teeth to.

I Want to Scream

I want to scream
I want to yell
This PTSD is a Living Hell

Nights bring horrors
Not Precious Dreams
The night is endless
Or so it seems

I become alert all night
I forget my days
How can a man love life this way
In a crowded room I feel all alone
I am the "point man," in my own home

I want to scream
I want to yell
PTSD is a living Hell

I wake at night, and sleep by day
Living like this, how can me and my children play
And then "My Bride" who feels alone
Because as I sleep she tries by herself, to make
this house a home

I do not want to be like this
God help me be the "me"
From whom she sought a lover's kiss

I want to scream
I want to yell
PTSD is a living Hell

I Want to Scream (Cont.)

Yes it's the memories, the war in the sand
Things that happened in that distant land
It is the hurt and the pain
It is the injuries I sustained

It is friends that I think of each day
Friends that bombs literally "blew" away
That is right, they are no longer here
It makes my heart ache and pain more severe

I want to scream
I want to yell
PTSD is a living HELL

Some nightmares are not memories at all
Some are dreams of my enemy I recall
Dreams of me still standing tall
Back in Iraq to kill them; to watch them all fall

I want to scream
I want to yell
PTSD is a living HELL

I do not want to be like this
God help me be the me that my loved ones miss

All Over Again

If I had to do it all over again
I would not dodge the call

I would not try to get out of my Duty
I would go back standing Proud & Tall

But if I had the choice of how I would return
If I had any input at all

Rather than come home a burden
With a screwed up head

I would rather complete my duties
Every one of my missions

And come home dead instead

It is a rotten thing to have said
A selfish thought to wish to be dead

To exit "Stage Left" and leave loved ones behind
Burdened with sadness and troubles of mine

All Over Again (Cont.)

I'll stick around
I'll ride this out

I am damn angry
I want to yell out loud

I hate being broken
It is not me

There are those I love
Who do not like this injured and handicapped me

It sucks and is a thought
I hate having at all

Yet if I had to do it
All over again

I would not dodge the call

I would report for duty
Standing "Proud and Tall"

"<u>Stateside</u>"

Fifteen days later found me "Stateside"
Extensive medical testing would reveal
How extensive the damage to my body
So many injuries to try to heal

The mission that was my last
A walk through hell for sure
With this Road of Recovery
I have another trip thru hell to endure

The Doctors are all talking
Of things I do not understand
Because of the injuries I endured
In that damned distant land of sand

They say that it may take some years
To fully comprehend
The extent of my Brain Damage
This news fills my eyes with tears

So many other injuries
Each will take some time
My body will never be the same
Neither will my mind

"Stateside" (Cont.)

It makes me mad as hell
That my body is now my jail
I do not fully understand
All the damage from the last blast
Sparked by my enemies hand

I am angry
I want back what was mine
I do not want to be broken the rest of my life
I want to go back and take an "Eye for an Eye"

My wife and children do not know
This broken man that they see
I do not know him either
I do not like this new me
And it is surely hell doing all these therapies

Where I will end up I do not know
Right now I do not have a clue
I do not know the way to go
It will no doubt be a long Recovery Road

The road it will be painful and seem so very slow
I will surly miss my uniform and combat boots
As I travel down this road
For I travel now in civilian shoes
With each and every step I go

"Stateside" (Cont.)

At least I am with my family now
So as I travel down this road
I know that I am not alone
For I am surrounded now by the love of home

Our Family... all eight of us!

"You have never truly lost something until you have lost something that you can never replace. Something that was not manufactured, that was not bought, that you would fight with all that was in you to keep. Those things are precious few: a True Love, a True Friend, a Spouse, a Child, a Dear Relative, a Brother in Arms, and FREEDOM!"

-Gordon Ewell

From Iraq

All Gave Some…

G.L. EWELL

Some Gave ALL!

My Last Mission

The mission we performed today
Was executed perfectly right through its dismal end
We found a half a dozen bombs along our route
Anyone would have killed a soldier or civilian
Of this I have no doubt

We even found a stash of unarmed bombs
They call a stash of bombs or weapons a cache
Enough heavy artillery rounds to make 24 more bombs
On any given day

Near the end of the mission
Something just was not right
Something was out of place
Something not noticeable at first sight

We stopped to interrogate
To take a closer look
To explore the uneasy gut feelings
That you learn to pay attention to
Though they're never mentioned in any training books

Sure enough a closer look revealed
Things were not as they should be
Things were distorted and out of place
That the untrained would never see

<u>My Last Mission (Cont.)</u>

We begin to do what we do best
To hunt, probe and explore
For the hidden danger that puts too many to a final rest
Sending our beloved Soldiers to knock at heaven's door

We found a hidden wire
Leading to a pile of debris and weeds
We knew disguised hell's fury and hell's fire
Another of the terrorist's "planted seeds"

We got in a "Battle Stance" like we had trained for
Prepared for other dangers as there is always more
They accompany the IEDs
To protect the enemies dirty little deeds
Deeds seldom reported on from this dirty little war

A man upon a roof top
Where no man should be
His head popping up and down
Obviously watching us, not liking what he sees

A bomb is right there waiting, just a few feet away
We found the death the enemy wanted to unleash today
Time is not on our side, this we know too well
The bomb is armed and patiently waiting
To blow us all to hell

<u>My Last Mission (Cont.)</u>

Before it can be disarmed
The enemy on the roof reacts
He touches his end of the wires to a small battery pack
This provided a tiny little spark
That ignited the bomb and made my world go dark

My vehicle now disabled
Filled with smoke too thick to see
I know too well what's coming next
As the enemy's target now is me

Stuck inside the vehicle
Now a fire filled jail
Enemy machine gun bullets
Rain down upon our prison cell

The streaking tail of a rocket
Rips across the sky
It just misses the vehicle behind me
The enemy's aim was high

A battle tank at a checkpoint up the road
Heard the fury of the bomb explode
And knew exactly what to do
He came to our aid and engaged the enemy too

My Last Mission (Cont.)

Sixty-four tons of iron and guns
The enemy fears and can't out run
His big guns fire and put an end
To the death intended for me and my friends

When the bomb exploded
Everyone knew just what to do
Though we lost a vehicle
We saved the entire crew

No one died in the blast
Though some were wounded, including me
This mission will be my last
As my body just cannot take another blast

Six times before in missions past
I have been blown up in a blast
Number seven now is different as I instantly knew
It is just too much for my body to get through

This time the pounding in my head
It just will not subside
My neck, shoulders and back all feel
Like they are burning up inside

My Last Mission (Cont.)

My eyes have fogged up
Clear images I no longer see
Another blast-induced nose bleed
But this time I cannot stop or slow down the bleed

Something is very wrong with me
Something serious for sure
My ears just won't stop ringing
Staying conscious such a difficult chore
I know I have a left leg, but I feel it no more

I've seen a single blast
Take the life of a brother
His last breath not much more a single gasp
Six times before I've walked away
This time number seven will be my last

Blast number seven, my last mission
Another walk through hell for sure
The grim reaper I have cheated yet once more
Again I have walked right by death's wide open door

I'm looking for Bombs, Improvised Explosive Devices (IEDs), from the window of my bomb hunting vehicle.

While Looking Out My Window

While looking out my window I See:

Blast holes in the road
Trash along the road
Weeds overtaking what were once fertile fields
And palm trees so dusty that they are brown…

And Snakes

I see the Enemy trying to kill me
Firefights
Bullets hitting armor near my head
Rocket Propelled Grenades being shot at me
And Bombs
And Blood
And Death
And more Bombs

These things are…
UGLY

While looking out my window I have seen:

Big pretty doves and multi-colored pheasants
Some humbling sunsets
The rise of a giant full red moon
And the smiles of little children I hope will know peace
In a land that could be so fertile
If all this needless fighting would cease

<u>While Looking Out My Window (Cont.)</u>

These things are…
Not as beautiful as you my Love
Or the thoughts I am having of you right this moment!

While looking for bombs out of my window, I see:
You babe…
I always see you

While looking for bombs out of my window, I have seen:
Angry Mobs
A society that has known hatred for far too long
Cowardly lazy men that treat their women like cattle
Destruction of homes and farms and businesses
By suicide bombers
And Bombs
And children playing soccer around a bomb on their
Soccer field
And Death
And more Bombs…

These things are …
UGLY

While looking for bombs out of my window, I see:
The possibility for a brighter future for these people

And I see…
You babe…
I ALWAYS See You My Love

One Day Closer

I lose track of the date
From each night to new day

But it really doesn't matter
While I am away

All I really need to know
With each new sunrise

Is that I am one day closer
To looking into your beautiful eyes

And to chasing our dreams together
Across heaven's eternal skies

Back in our home
Being your man

Back by your side
Holding your hand

Back being a father like I used to
You have filled my role long enough

I need to come home and relieve you

Your burdens are many
Your load it is plenty

You are doing a great job
There is so much that you do

One Day Closer (Cont.)

I can't say it enough
I sincerely "Thank-You"

God knows I miss you and the kids too
It makes days hard and me feel so "blue"

I lose track of the days
Yes, it is true

But all I really need to know
Is with each new sunrise

I am one day closer
To looking into your beautiful eyes

The Beautiful Eyes of my "Luv-bug."

<u>Red, White and Blue</u>

This war makes me so angry, that all I see is *"Red"*

It gets me so frustrated, I can't keep thoughts
straight in my head

But then a light shines through and I can
hold my head up high

For I fight with all my might, for the things
I know are right

Like our "love" so pure and bright
and my arms wrapped around you tight

This is what I can see, in the light so soft and *"White"*

That vision of you "my love," is so beautiful and true

It makes the color change again, for now I
see the color *"Blue"*

That's the color that my heart feels, when I
am not next to you

I ache so very badly, being away from you
that deep inside my heart I feel totally *"Blue"*

I feel *"Blue"* slowly fill me, from my head
down to my toes

Depression knows no boundaries, wherever I go it goes

<u>Red, White and Blue (Cont.)</u>

But then a twinkling star, I see up in the sky

It reminds me of "your beauty"
and of the "sparkle" in your eyes

Your picture I put near my heart, as I profess
eternal love to you

Then I get all giggly thinking, of all the "love grotto"
dancing we will do

When I return back home to you, and lye next
to you in our bed

Now I see our hearts on fire, I see our lovers *"Red"*

Our passions will burn brighter, than
the brightest flame

The intensity of which, nothing could tame
or ever change

But damn, I can't act out my passions
with you in our bed

Oh here comes a color change again, now I am back to
where I started; back to my anger *"Red"*

Anger will be my battle cry, as I kick some sand
in someone's eye

<u>Red, White and Blue (Cont.)</u>

Perhaps then I will see the soft *"White"* light

That will give way to thoughts of our love, so
pure and right

I want you "my love," every day and each
and every night

But right now "my love," we know
that this cannot be so

Hurry; come see the *"White"* light
see it now, there it goes

Well welcome back, old color *"Blue"*
and your old friend "depression" too

My night time mission now is through
we found some bombs, and saved a few

Got in a fire fight, and apprehended suspects too
all while bomb hunting and enforcing the curfew

I have the time I need to entertain the "both of you"

I am just way too tired, and I don't want to

I don't care if you decide to stay
just keep off to yourselves, I need some sleep today

G.L. EWELL

<u>Again</u>

Again I see that blinding light
Feel the air get sucked out of my chest and lungs
Feel the heat of an intense fireball
Hear the sound of thunder louder than Artillery guns

Like a rag doll with no control
Once again I am tossed about
I try to shout out a "Status"
For a moment no sound comes out

Pounding in my head clear down to my toes
The deafening ringing in my ears
The smell of burning hydraulic hose
Again the smell of burning hair
And one more bloody nose

Once again that shooting pain
Running down my neck and spine
Like a current of high voltage electricity
It doesn't feel so very fine
In fact it hurts like Hell and it gets worse every time

Again the flash of panic
As I wonder about my crew
With all the smoke inside, I cannot even see my driver
I need to verify that they are all ok too

<u>Again (Cont.)</u>

Once again the sounds of bullets
That comes from Enemy guns
Disabled my vehicle is their target now
It isn't any fun

Once again I was just "Blown-Up"
By an Enemy Improvised Explosive Device
A hazard of being a "Bomb Hunter"
That just isn't very nice

But that is my mission
That is the job I do
If that bomb detonated on any other vehicle
It would have killed at least one Soldier maybe two

The rest of the patrol swiftly executes a Battle Drill"
Rehearsed both in hot blazing suns and dark of night
They are executed flawlessly, as they join the firefight
Now the Enemy is on the run, quickly taking flight

The hazards of being a "Bomb Hunter"
They are dangerous for sure
But knowing lives were spared tonight
Will make my personal pain worth suffering for

"Barking"

The 50 cal. is "barking" tonight
It doesn't "speak" without an Enemy in sight

My turn to sleep, but sleep won't come
Not while listening to the sound of that gun

Though not afraid, I cannot close my eyes
Or quiet the shaking that I feel inside

I want to get up, take weapon in hand
Head out to the perimeter, take aim, and watch blood
cover the sand

I do not have a desire to kill on this eve
Nor a desire to sleep while the Enemy is trying to
terminate me

He does not know or care for that for which I stand
He has no idea why I am here in "His Land"

It is certainly not that I like what I see
It is because I believe these people deserve to be free

"Barking" (Cont.)

I have NOT forgotten 9/11 and the thousands of lives
lost at the feet of Lady Liberty
You're damn right I have my reasons for wanting
to bring the Enemy to his knees
Begging for forgiveness and mercy from me

I have my training, my mission, my orders you see
As long as he is armed, my mercy will be in the form of
a light "trigger squeeze"
A prayer on my lips, not for his "new start"
But that my bullet will find and explode his cold heart

I'll pray he dies hard and in Death still finds pain
I hope there he finds no virgins, only Hell's eternal
"Ball and Chain"

The 50 cal. is "barking" out loud tonight
For the Enemy that "bark" will have a very big "bite"

I feel it a welcome invitation to me
to come join the fight
To be trying to sleep, just doesn't feel right
So try all I want, with all my might
It is a lost cause; there will be no sleep for me tonight

"Barking" (Cont.)

The 50 cal. is "barking" out loud tonight
It does not "bark" without an Enemy in sight

The "barking" believe me is a welcome sound
While sleep won't come, that "barking" means I can at
least safely lie down

Note: In this poem, the reference to a "50 cal." is referring to a 50 caliber Machine Gun. It is a "crew serve" weapon, meaning under normal conditions a "crew" of two men would operate the weapon; one firing it and one feeding it ammunition. It is a very large and effective weapon.

Above is an example of an Improvised Explosive Device (IED) or commonly a "Roadside bomb." Two Heavy Artillery Shells were wired to a Long Range Cordless Telephone Base Station and a small battery pack, buried under a small amount of dirt against a curb. As a target gets close, someone calls the base station which instead of ringing provides the "spark" that ignites, or rather explodes the Artillery shells.

Bombs

Roadside bombs are the Enemies weapon of choice
Their effects are so devastating
They are hidden literally everywhere
Everyone is armed and waiting

Waiting to unleash their devastating power
Upon our Soldiers at any given time or hour
They care not if it's night or day
They'll lie in wait for many hours
For our Soldiers to come their way
So that they can "Blow" them away

Those who activate and hide them
They do not value life
They could care less how many lives are lost
If they can kill a Soldier it is worth the cost

The price that is paid by innocent children everyday
Who happen to get killed just walking by one
While on their way to play
The Enemy simply does not care
If civilians die, just for being there

Bombs (Cont.)

There where the bomb was selectively placed
Right where a soldier or his vehicle
Might have to stop, to pause, or hesitate
It does not matter if it is a busy market place
The Enemy would gladly watch everyone die
Just to witness one soldier have death in his eyes

For a "Westerner" it is a hard concept to understand
How one could be so calloused to not value life at all
Not even the lives of "their own" in their "Homeland"
All the Enemy cares about is executing their plan

"Innocent Civilians" and "Collateral Damage"
are terms that "Westerners" use
The Enemy sees it as a point of weakness and
does not care one bit at all
As long as he can witness our Soldiers fall

The bombs come in all shapes and sizes
Many are often so very well disguised
They simply cannot be seen thru "untrained eyes"
That is why experts like me must find them before
they can release all the death they hold inside

<u>Bombs (Cont.)</u>

The bombs are set off in so many ways
By cordless telephone bases, two way radios, cell phones,
pressure switches and more
The list seems as endless as calendar days
And is limited only by imagination in so many ways
Even hair thin strands of copper wire
Which run from the bomb to the Enemy, who will
touch the wire to a battery post, and then he will smile

Thinking of this makes me proud of those
who will hunt him down
And turn his fat cheesy smile into a permanent frown

But for now MY focus must remain on solely one thing
Finding bombs and ensuring other "Bomb Hunters" are all aware
Of the very best tactics and techniques to use while
"hunting" for all the bombs "out there"
So routes and roads will be as safe as can be
For Soldiers and Civilians to travel behind
"Route Clearance Experts," just like me

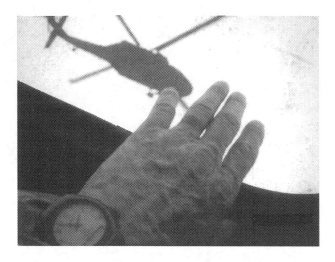

A Blackhawk helicopter takes me off on a new mission.

The End of My Day

The end of my day has finally drawn near

The problem with that, is you are not here

Not here to kiss, to touch and to feel

Not here to remind me that you Love me still

I take that back I am glad you are not

This place is HELL and not just because it is hot

However I long to be close to you

And wish that you were near

So I could hold you close to me

And nibble on your ear

Our love it is so very strong

I long to hold you all night long

All wrapped up tightly in my arms

The End of My Day (Cont.)

With your head laying upon my chest

I am positive we both could rest

And sleep the whole night away

When we awoke we would make time for a little play

Loving thoughts I have enjoyed but now I must rest

Tomorrow's mission is a difficult one

I'll need to be at my best

I have your picture near my heart

And one of our children too

Don't worry love I am fine

Who I worry about is you

One thing is constant, never ending and true

That is my "honorable, faithful and everlasting"

Love for only YOU

Combat Engineer

When I'm around, "Boots on the ground"
Only the Enemy needs to fear
Expertly trained and skilled, I am here
With my men and with my gear

I am a Combat Engineer

My mission will get done right
With the Enemy in my sight
By day or night
I'm fit to fight

I am a Combat Engineer

I'll build a bridge to get to town
Or blow one up, to slow things down
The Enemy won't stand a chance tonight
My Squad is here to win the fight

We are Combat Engineers

We don't mess around, aren't here for fun
The Enemy had better run
If he gets in my sight
He will die tonight

I am a Combat Engineer

He can "plant a bomb"
But I'll come along
And to his demise
I will disarm his disguise

Combat Engineer (Cont.)

I am a Combat Engineer

So rest tonight, we will protect this site
We will save your house and home
The Enemy won't dare to fight
He knows out here we own the night
With all our might, even with our life
We will win the fight and give you back
Your human rights

WE ARE COMBAT ENGINEERS

G.L. EWELL

Essayons!
(meaning "Let Us Try!")

The hand on the end of the hydraulic arm looks like a big pitchfork, and digs like a shovel. It is called a "spork." In 2006 the insurgents were offering a One Million Dollar reward to anyone who could bring them the hand off a Buffalo. They NEVER got one!

The vehicle is 27' long 13' tall and weighs 26 tons. It takes skilled drivers to maneuver the crowded streets.

The Buffalo patrolling for bombs in a Baghdad suburb.

The RG-31 usually has a crew of four. It is an armored 10-ton vehicle normally used in Route Clearance to provide security for the "Buffalo" and its crew.

An RG-31 after getting "blown up" by an IED.

Pre-War

Oil Painting of my wife (Terra) and I painted by an
Iraq Artist, in Baghdad from a small wallet photo I
carried with me. It was taken at a Military Ball just
one year prior to my deployment to Iraq (the original
oil painting measures 2' 6" in height, is 2' wide and
in color).

Kiss Upon the Wind

I have placed a kiss
Upon the wind

I pray it finds
The right door to go in

And once inside
I pray it finds the room

That is lighted by
Your lovely face

And when it finds
Your luscious lips

Upon them I pray
You will feel my kiss

With the same pure love
I have for you

With which it left
My finger tips

Breath of Life

The very thought of you
My dear love

Is the sweetness
I taste on my lips

As the breath of life
That fills my lungs

Created by your
Precious gift of love

Passes over them softly
Like the wind beneath a dove

And allows my heart to beat
Stronger than anything on water or land

I patiently wait
To hold your hand

While love enriched blood
Pumps through my body

To feed my muscles
To feed my brain

To give me Strength for us
And knowledge that I will retain

That you're Love for me will never change
That in love, we will always remain

Star Filled Sky

Star filled sky
Moon so bright
Please shine your light
On "My Love" tonight

Oh how I wish
With all my might
To hold her in my arms, so tight
Not just for a moment, but night after night

As we melt into each other by the candlelight
Gently placed upon her thighs
Are soft, wet kisses meant to tantalize
While my love begins to swell and rise

When we make love
It feels so right
Like heaven above
It is pure delight

I will look deep into her eyes
And softly whisper "there's no need to cry"
I'll remind her I am hers, not just this night
But for the rest of her entire life

As well as beyond
The star filled sky

The star filled sky
That watches over us each night

Eternal Love

Yes roses are red

And yes, violets are blue

Still more beautiful is that Our Love

Is Eternal and True

Being apart is painful

Each day I feel blue

It is dizzying the hurt

I feel in my head

Not to mention my heart

That feels broken in two

And eyes that tear up when

I think of you

But then I can smile

For a bright light shines through

The one that reminds me Our Love

Is Eternal and True

Your G.I. Joe

Yes, I am your G.I. Joe

Off to a distant land I must go

I'll do my duty

With honor and pride

And each day I'll wish

I was home by your side

Many things I'll see through

My "missing you" brown eyes

However, beautiful visions of you will

Always be my guiding light

Yes Sweetheart, I Love You

Try your best to not be blue

Knowing that I will forever be

Faithful and true

Each and every second that

I am away from you!

Apple Tree Love

First came Adam, followed by Eve

Then came an apple

And a man with a mission to deceive

Some called him Lucifer, I Prefer Steve

Steve made an offer that Eve thought was swell

This proves she was a blonde, for now we know Hell

So far I've just rambled, as I'm sure you can tell

There is a reason I've written this poem for you

A reason I wanted to be sure that you knew

That reason of course, is that I LOVE YOU

So why all the rambling and nonsense above

Well it was just an attempt to express that I would walk
through hell for your love

I'll love you forever, and you'll love me

We are like a hand in a glove, fit just perfectly

But just for insurance, to leave nothing to chance
I don't believe I'll ever plant us an apple tree

BUS WINDOW

From the window of this bus
I view America's heartland

On the way to Fort Riley
For some training before
Heading to the sand

I'm wondering how I could
Possibly be smiley

It's because I LOVE YOU, and my
Heart is in your hands

Me and my "Tea," at our Maverick Beach.

What a good looking couple!

Our Kids
(From left: Jaime, Cory, Kenny, Scarlett,
Lincoln and Shelby).

Our Sunday Dress

Dressed for the Holidays.

"Gordy-isims," are random thoughts and quotes by me. All are original; the good and bad. They began as I told myself every morning I had to try to write down something positive... Even on days I hurt like hell!

SECTION TWO

"GORDY-ISMS"

Whether you see the glass "half empty," or "half full,"
if you are thirsty, be smart enough to drink it!

I was thinking of a list of most powerful weapons. I think these are top of my list. Sharpest Weapon is the tongue; Most Powerful and Mighty is the Pen; Best Shield is a Memory; And the most efficient is a helping hand. We all have them and can decide whether we use our weapons to do good works or to cause harm.

It is fun to look for Angels. They are quite easy to spot for me. The secret is not to look for wings, but rather someone doing a kind deed.

People are a lot like roses. To fully embrace and appreciate a rose, it is inevitable that at some time a thorn will prick you. Thorns do not take away from the beauty of a rose. You just have to take in stride, that while enjoying roses, every now and then, you will get "pricked."

Some of the world's most beautiful flowers bloom from the most obnoxious weeds. I guess we sometimes just need to have the patience to "grow" thru some of life's "un-pleasantries," to get to a point where we can enjoy "our" own beautiful bloom.

To really get the most out of life, we need to nurture relationships with those in our life. It is easy to find fault with anyone. But if you look for the good qualities, and compliment on them, you may be pleasantly surprised that you will see more of them.

Kind words and actions both have the same roots… Kind Thoughts!

What seems to make people seen to gravitate towards others that they would like to be around? If you take a closer look, I believe you will find it is NOT money, stocks, or large estates. I believe you will find it is laughter, kindness and love.

Believe it or not, there IS a way that everyone can actually "See into the Future." All one has to do is simply look into the eyes of someone that is really "Down on Their Luck," that you opt to do a random act of kindness for. You will be able to see a soul that will truly be edified and full of gratitude, well into the "future," for a very long time!

Doing math this morning I realized that when we help others, we SUBTRACT from our own problems; We ADD, to our feelings of happiness; our individual worries appear to get DIVIDED in half; while our blessings are instantly MULTIPLIED.

When all else seems to fail, make a call! Call home, phone a friend, dial a crisis hotline... There is ALWAYS someone who wants to hear from you; one person in particular and the communication line is ALWAYS open! To access it, all you have to do, is open your heart, and take a knee.

How would you explain the beautiful smell of a rose to someone who could not smell? Or describe the magnificent array of colors in a brilliant sunset, to one who has never had sight? How to relate the sweet taste of sugar to one that has never tasted it? I believe not all things that touch our hearts need words to pass them long. Some things are best conveyed with a simple Hug, a tender touch, or an "I Love You!"

Perception is a funny thing. Every now and then we come across someone we think really needs our help. Usually the timing isn't the best, and after a quiet "grumble," we tend to lend a helping hand. Funny thing is when the deed is said and done, and we realize how good we now feel. Then comes the realization of who was really helped; that the real angel, was one we asked for.

Time is so precious. We know in a day, there is not enough to accomplish all that we would like. When we give time in service of others, we freely give away one of our most precious commodities. Whether you give your time to your favorite charity, to help a friend, neighbor, or a simple act of kindness to a stranger; you give a gift that is precious; and I promise that is time WELL spent!

It doesn't matter if you see the glass as "half empty," or "half full." If you are thirsty, be smart enough to drink it! Either way it will quench your thirst, and that should give you something to smile about.

Letters, by themselves are hardly noticeable. Properly paired and linked together become words and have meaning. Words, assembled together in the right order become sentences; having behind them definition, depth and meaning can promote healing to the sick, start a revolution, or break a lovers heart. We have the power to assemble our words for good or bad every single day.

Random acts of kindness remind me of lightning... they often take but mere seconds to have a very powerful effect, they are always impressive, can give you a chill that makes the hair on your neck stand up and warm your heart at the same time, and are always welcomed and refreshing, like a soft gentle summer rain, that can follow lightning.

The War on Terrorism has taken a tremendous toll on so many. Not just in Soldier lives that have been directly or indirectly lost (giving the Ultimate price for Freedom), but also with the Wounded, Families, and Caregivers as well. In my own case, I was Severely Wounded. However, NOT totally disabled... Rather, I was given an opportunity from a "Higher Power," to enjoy seeing life from a different point of view.

You may not get all you want out of life, but you can put everything you want into it and if you do it with caring treatment of others in mind, you will get back more than your heart can hold, of the things in life that are really important!

I may not hear birds sing anymore, but I hear every word someone speaks out of Love; I may not see someone roll their eyes at me, because I am slow to walk behind, but I see everyone that could use MY Help. I may not be able to feel my feet, but I can "Feel" the warmth in my heart, that comes from helping others. Have an ache you want to disappear, do something for someone else, your ache will go away, even if only for a moment, it's a good moment!

It is not often that a person finds a true friend. Someone who wants nothing more form him than an ear to listen, a shoulder for a tear to land on, a laugh at a good joke, even a laugh at a bad joke, and the knowledge that they would do anything for you, often before you would even have to ask.

What is history but a small unit with which to measure time? Unless you unleash your entire treasure chest of God given talent, tireless effort and endless love into it. Then and only then is born a tiny "moment of everlasting greatness." A moment that in itself has the potential to forever change a life, yours or perhaps the life of someone else and you may never even know it "at the time."

There is a difference between having a big ego and being self-confident. Egos have to be fed, and have to come first. A "self-confident soul," uses talents to "feed others," and eats last. I hate big egos. They don't look good on anyone.

Tonight, I will not complain about the pain in my legs, as my friend who lost his, would love to feel my pain. I won't complain about my bed, rather smile, remembering I didn't have to "hand sweep" sand off of it. In the morning, I won't complain if I can't sleep in. Rather, I will be grateful I don't need to check my boots for scorpions before I put my feet in them. I'll enjoy a sunrise without the sound of mortar rounds nearby. I'll say a prayer for my brothers and sisters who are still in harm's way.

I truly believe that "Knowledge is Power," and that "the Pen is Mightier than the Sword." To keep from getting "dehydrated," I have to actively water my "thinker." One thing I try is letting the dictionary "flop" open, and picking one new word definition to learn, and try to use it on someone during the day. If occasionally I pick a word that could get "my beak broke," I do allow myself to "pick" again.

Seen an ad for sunless tanning today... I can "Fake Bake" my skin, I could dye my hair, or even change the colors of my eyes with contact lenses... all are temporary. To make a change that will make a difference must come from within, from your heart. If you want to really feel good, and project a radiant glow that will get noticed, try a simple act of random kindness. The results will last longer than your fake tan.

"Life is like a box of Chocolates" (Forrest Gump). So true! If we do nothing with them, they could all melt, and become nothing more than a great big messy, sticky, rotten, glob of goop. If you want to really enjoy "Life's Chocolates" before they melt, run around and share the box of chocolate with your family and friends. Then, you will really "enjoy" every single one!

The "wealth of my heart," "happiness," "self-worth," however you phrase it, you feel at your very best, not by looking in your wallet, purse, or at your bank statement; but rather by leading with your heart, taking risks and doing your best, to be the best friend you can be. Often it is a close friend who is the recipient of "your best," works. It could also be the good fortune, if you choose it, to let the recipient be a total stranger.

Everyone has heard the expression "home is where your heart is." But it often takes graduating from the school of "Hard Knocks," before one realizes that place will never actually be a "Physical Address."

Sleep did not come again tonight. Though I do not hear the War anymore, I still SEE it, even with just "One Eye." I see faces twisted up with Pain, Heartache, Exhaustion, and Fear... Faces with the never ending stare of Death upon them... Guess I'll go start coffee. Today is a new day, and a chance to see the glass as "Half Full," rather than "Half Empty!"

There is a saying that says "To change the world, you must start with yourself" (unknown). I believe that. However, since 90% of Americans never travel outside America, let alone the state they live in; I say why try to change the world. Why not first make a change in your own community! All it takes is a small investment of time, to have a BIG impact!

Volunteerism, Community Involvement, and Accountability of Elected Officials; Too often I hear people complain about the way people are "running their community." Yet a few gentle questions will reveal that the complainer, did not vote, does not attend city council, or town hall meetings, and is not involved in volunteering at all. Strong Communities, thrive upon involvement and participation from everyone!

Today the same two roads greet me. I can choose to let my aches, pains, and things I have lost, bog me down, and drag me down the path of "self-pity;" or, I can choose to be grateful for WHAT and WHO I have in my life and travel the other path, where I know I can always find a treasure along the way. It's time to paint on a smile, and start looking for treasure.

"Things that matter... things which don't..." No matter how many lists or revisions of lists I make, when you get right down to it, life is all about people, and our interactions with them. Loved ones, friends, and neighbors... want to be rich, take care of all of them.

Last year, for the second in a row, Soldier Suicides killed more Servicemen and Women than the enemy did in Afghanistan and Iraq combined. Last night, while my PTSD and "petty" problems kept me up all night, again, at least 8 of my "Brothers and Sisters" allowed their demons to KILL them! Today I will thank God my "demons" were kept "at bay," and pray that today, someone notices a Soldier in distress!

Some days, all that motivates me is the knowledge that I had better not complain; because I KNOW others far worse off than I. I also know they do not complain near as much as some who have things 100 times better off than them. Their example humbles me, as well as gives me a reminder that I need only focus on ME, and not judge others on either side of the pendulum from where I am.

It is a fact that stupid laws get passed, often because a small minority of "Village Idiots," is SMART enough to come together, unite, rally, pester their Congressional Representative and VOTE! All while the MAJORITY, who are ABSOLUTELY against the "Proposed Legislation" sit back, do NOTHING, is absent from the polling booths at home saying "Hell that will NEVER pass." When it passes, then who are the "Village Idiots?" Get involved people!

Why? Because I can do it; because I want to; because I am free to do it; because it is the right thing to do and I will feel good doing it… helping someone. Try it!

In your "Light" dear God, allow me to learn from my past and apply it to my Future. I'll strive to be a better man tomorrow than today; that I may rest easier tonight.

Trust is the cornerstone of any relationship. A business deal or a passionate love, there has to be trust at the foundation. Otherwise the business deal will fall through or the fire of love will burn out. The best we can do is to be honest in all our affairs, business or love. It won't soften the pain if the other party "does wrong," but at least you will have the satisfaction of knowing that you did not throw a stone at a "glass house."

There are politicians who want to cut Veteran benefits. Currently, only 2% to 4% of the population of America has ever served in the military (use whichever stat you want). Of that small percentage, 18 soldiers are committing suicide every day. If politicians want to cut Veteran benefits so bad, all they need to do, is the Pathetic… "NOTHING!" The alarmingly high suicide rate will begin to cut the budget for them! Our Veterans deserve better than "NOTHING!"

Afterword

I was recognized by Utah State Governor Jon Huntsman at his "State of the State" address to our State Leaders and the citizens of Utah at our State Capital Building. My oldest daughter Shelby is just over my right shoulder.

No one comes back from a war the same man or woman they were before they left. No matter how badly one wants to believe that they escaped unscathed, the truth is, every single soldier leaves a war scared.

A Soldier does not have to be injured by the hand of the enemy to be scared. Just because a Soldier in a war zone did not see or experience "combat action" first hand, does not mean they have not experienced trauma.

Mortar and Rocket attacks on our bases, in both Afghanistan and Iraq, have at times been deadly. In one such attack in Mosul, Iraq a dining facility was directly hit. Many Soldiers died. Many more were severely wounded. Many soldiers, whose duties would not normally put them outside the perimeter of the base, where contact with the enemy would be a high probability and could happen anywhere, any place at any time; if not wounded, were witness to the trauma that ensued. They were "First Responders" to attempt to aid and evacuate the wounded, as well as to fight the fire and reduce other dangers that were secondary as a direct result of the attack. These Soldiers were affected and to some degree, traumatized by this event.

Doctors, Nurses, Medics and other Soldiers, whose duties are working at aid stations and hospitals, receiving wounded from the "battle field" are definitely affected and traumatized by what they see on a daily basis. They see Soldiers arriving daily with wounds that are very severe. Soldiers who have often lost limbs, have been engulfed by deadly fires, suffering 2nd and 3rd degree burns over the majority of their bodies and are barely recognizable... How could one not be affected?

How could anyone witness horrors like that daily and not be affected. The administrators who need to try to interview these wounded soldiers, or the supply personnel who try to gather and collect personal belongings, like wallets, photos, wedding rings, un-mailed letters home or journals, to be forwarded to the wounded Soldiers at hospitals back in Germany or America, or worse to the soldiers "next of kin;" how can anyone think these soldiers are not traumatized to some degree?

The reality is every Soldier, to some degree, experiences trauma deployed to a theater of war.

There is no such thing as a "Linier Battlefield" with the gorilla like tactics used in "Urban Warfare." The enemy dresses like the civilians, hides among civilians, attacks from within groups of civilians and uses them for shields… human shields. It is the ugliest type of warfare. Anyone who is involved, directly or indirectly is traumatized to some degree. Which means literally, that EVERY soldier deployed to a these theaters of war, is affected by trauma to some degree. Whether it is by a firsthand experience being directly engaged with the enemy, being wounded, caring for the wounded, witnessing a traumatic event, or even repeatedly hearing stories of traumatic events, all can cause a degree of trauma.

In essence, no one returns from war, the same person they were when they left. Everyone needs to understand this. Including the Soldier who believes they are the same person they were before they deployed to war.

Until this realization comes, so many needing help will never get it. Until this realization comes, how this harsh reality will continue to manifest itself will be in the continued increasing statistics of Domestic Violence, Drug and Alcohol Abuse, Divorce, Suicide and Severe Depression among the ranks of such a "Special" group of Americans… the "American Soldier."

Less than two percent of our entire population is serving in our Armed Services. Less than two percent of our population willing to shoulder the burden of defending our freedoms whenever and wherever called upon.

We as a nation owe it to these people to ensure they are taken care of. Not just to take care of physical wounds, but mental scars of war as well.

We as a nation owe it to the families of these warriors, to take care of the families as well. They too are suffering. They too have scars and trauma from war. Their lives have also been adversely affected. Many are now in the unasked for roles of life long caregivers for their Soldier and they need to be taken care of, trained, and receive benefits for taking on the role and not running from it.

It is my sincere desire that if you are troubled, do not be afraid or ashamed to ask for help. If you know someone who you think is suffering, do not be afraid to intervene, either directly or indirectly. A phone call could save a life. Above all know that help is out there! HELP IS AVAILABLE! Please do not let yourself, or someone you know suffer, and go without.

My Prayer for My Military Family

A prayer Dear Lord I ask of thee
Be with and protect our Soldiers wherever they may be
Be with their loved ones, for they need you too
Fill their hearts with your sweet love
That they may have peace, I humbly ask this of you

For those who suffer from wounds and scars of war
Ease their pain Lord and place an angel at their door

For those who just don't understand
I pray give them knowledge and compassion
That they may be able to offer a helping hand

For those who feel lost and know not what to do
Show them the way Dear Lord
To those that can give them help and guidance too

Bless the Caregivers and those who are Volunteers
Let them know their work is needed and so very dear

Don't let anyone get turned away
For those who need it, find them a place to stay

This prayer Dear Lord I humbly ask of thee
Be with our Soldiers, Veterans and their Families Lord
Wherever they may be
Amen…

No explanation needed… Love.

In Iraq 2006.

About the Author

Master Sergeant (MSG) Gordon L. Ewell was born on June 8th, 1967 in Nephi, Utah. He graduated from Emery County High School in May 1985 and joined the Utah Army National Guard on August 28, 1985 with initial assignment to the 1457th Engineer Battalion as a Combat Engineer. In August 1991, he transitioned to the Active Guard Reserve program, with Delta Company, of the 1457th Engineer Battalion.

His 24 year career has been marked with distinction through notable accomplishments that render him an excellent example for other Soldiers to follow.

Throughout his outstanding military career he has served in key positions as Training and Administration Specialist, Supply Sergeant, Combat Engineer Squad Leader and Personnel Section Sergeant.

From Master Sergeant (MSG) Gordon L Ewell's initial entry into Military Service, his superiors recognized his outstanding initiative and a deep care for his fellow Soldiers. He has been recognized as one who would do whatever it takes to accomplish the mission, or help a fellow Soldier in need. His 24 year career has been marked with distinction through notable accomplishments. MSG Ewell has graduated from over 30 Army Resident Schools, graduating as the Honor Graduate, or in the top 10% of his class, from nearly every one of them.

He has completed, with a "Superior" rating, over 1,000 hours of Army Correspondence Training. Additionally, he earned an Associate of Science degree in April of 1999.

During his service in Iraq, MSG Ewell performed 59 challenging and dangerous missions, which involved both the coordination of Convoy Route Clearance and Route Clearance Observation missions, based upon his knowledge and expertise in these areas. MSG Ewell was vital in the creation of the first Route Clearance Handbook, and was further recognized by the Corps staff as the Multi-National Corps "Subject Matter Expert," in Route Clearance. His lessons learned in Iraq have been published in many Army periodicals.

MSG Ewell led over 33% of the missions he was on in Iraq. He was recognized by his superiors to be unparalleled in his physical stamina and toughness complemented with superior technical and tactical capabilities. This was clearly demonstrated on the battlefield when his efforts under heavy enemy fire were unrivaled, which earned him a Bronze Star Medal, the Purple Heart Medal, and the Combat Action Badge.

During his Combat Missions, on six separate occasions, a vehicle he was in was blown-up by Improvised Explosive Devices (IED's). One of the explosions was so powerful that it blew impacted wisdom teeth out the side of his jaw. In addition to major jaw damage, he suffers from broken vertebrae in his neck, damage to his lower spine, permanent loss of hearing (leaving him legally deaf).

He suffered the anatomical loss of his right eye and peripheral/ bi-lateral vision loss in his left eye, leaving him legally blind. He has a Traumatic Brain Injury (TBI), Flaccid Neurologic Bladder, loss of balance, an abnormal gait, and is fighting to overcome Post-Traumatic Stress Disorder (PTSD).

MSG Ewell returned from combat duty in December 2006, and assigned to the 640th Regiment (Regional Training Institute). Because of the severity of his combat injuries, he was Medically Retired from injuries sustained while at war, in February 2010.

His "Medical Journey" to date has included six major surgeries, treatment at Eight different hospitals, in three different states, by over 47 different Doctors, Surgeons, Specialists and other health care professionals; not counting the more than a dozen different Dentists, Endodontists, Oral Surgeons, and other Dental Specialists.

Today, though he is 100% disabled, he continues to serve with distinction, as a Member of the Blue Star Riders, as a Volunteer at the George E. Wahlen V.A. Hospital in Salt Lake City, with the Veterans of Foreign Wars, the Disabled American Veterans, and the American Legion.

The retired Master Sergeant currently resides in Eagle Mountain, Utah, with his wife Terra and their six children. He enjoys being a husband and a father and watching his babies grow.

He also enjoys public speaking and the Beach.

2

Military Awards and Decorations

Bronze Star Medal
Purple Heart Medal
Meritorious Service Medal
Army Commendation Medal (with Bronze Oak Leaf)
Army Achievement Medal
Army Good Conduct Medal (with 6 Bronze Knots)
Army Reserve Components Achievement Medal (with 3 Bronze Oak Leafs)
National Defense Service Medal (with Bronze Star)
Iraq Campaign Medal (with Campaign Star)
Global War on Terrorism Service Medal
Armed Forces Reserve Medal (with "M" Devise and Silver Hourglass)
NCO Professional Development Ribbon, (3rd Award)
Army Service Ribbon
Overseas Service Ribbon
Army Reserve Components Overseas Training Ribbon (3rd Award)
Combat Action Badge
Diver and Mechanic Badge (with wheeled vehicle clasp)
Sharpshooter Weapon Marksmanship Badge
Utah Commendation Medal (3rd award)
Utah 2002 Olympic Winter Games Service Ribbon
Utah Emergency Service Ribbon
Utah Achievement Ribbon
Utah Recruiting Ribbon
Utah Service Ribbon

Joint Meritorious Unit Award
Army Superior Unit Award

Noteworthy Civilian Awards Include:

City of Eagle Mountain Outstanding Citizenship Award (2007)

The State of Utah Department of Public Safety Executive Award of Merit:
In recognition and appreciation of extraordinary service and outstanding contributions on behalf of the citizens of Utah (2008)

His most treasured Titles and Accomplishments are:
Husband, Father, Son, Brother, Friend, Comrade, Patriot, Veteran and Volunteer.

The day I received my Purple Heart.

Rod and Marjory Ewell, my parents.

With "Wolf" Hamilton (right) Founder of the
Blue Star Riders and my dear friend.

Acknowledgments

To all men and women who have worn the uniform of a "Defender" of our country and her freedoms, I commend you! You are part of a very special and elite group of our Americans that currently is less than 2% of our nation's total population. That in itself makes you all a hero in my book!

To "Loved Ones," family and friends and anyone who has supported our country's Soldiers, Sailors, Airmen and Marines, and continues to support them… I sincerely thank you! You play a vital role in our nation's security, as without your support we could not do our mission and stay focused if we had constant worry or doubt about things on the "home front."

To those who have endured cold, dark nights in Europe's Black Forests; the cold bitter bite of a Korean Winter; the damp endless rains of Vietnam; the disease and humidity of dense jungles and island hoping throughout the pacific; the heat of Africa and Somalia; the terrain of Afghanistan and the blasting sand storms of Iraq, in battle, I Salute You! You have intestinal fortitude, endurance and courage beyond measure.

To my brothers and sisters, "Wounded Warriors" who are suffering mentally or physically, I have empathy for you. I suffer with you. Stay strong and never give up; continue the fight! Do not be too proud to take a "Hand Up" when offered it!

For those who "Gave All" I will never run out of tears.

A "Wounded Warrior," has little hope for success, if not surrounded by the love of family, the fellowship of friends, or the camaraderie of other Soldiers and Veterans.

Suicide is currently taking the lives of more of our Soldiers than the enemy is. This must stop! It is not acceptable! Why one makes the decision to travel that path, I do not pretend I have any answers. I doubt we will ever know, as the reasons are so varied from one individual to another. What I do think however, is perhaps we need to not put so much energy into asking "Why" and put more energy into looking for any sign at all that might indicate that someone is in need of help. Help is available. Unfortunately, for too many, they simply do not know where to find it. Money should NEVER be a factor in determining if a "Wounded Defender of Our Nation" receives treatment and care... physical or mental care!

I could not have progressed, or gotten back as much as I have were it not for so many people and organizations. In fact, I could fill a whole book full of those to whom I feel I will always owe a debt of thanks.

To everyone who has helped me or my family during my long and ongoing journey of recovery, thank-you. You know who you are and know also that I will never forget you kindness, your care, your bedside manner, financial support, listening ears (to lots of my anger and frustrations), and shoulders to not only lean against, but also to cry upon as I have learned to embrace and accept this new me. From the humble heart of a "broken old Warrior" I sincerely Thank-You All!

I cannot tell my family enough how much I love them! Tea, my "Beautiful Bride," it has been one hell of a journey. I have never stopped loving you, and never could have come this far without you. Thank God for the kids and "Our Beach!"

Mom and Dad, you continue to define "unconditional love." You have ensured I have always gotten where I need to be and what I need, and not once complained or asked for anything in return. Your sacrifices of both time and money have often left you little of both.

My dad spent 13 months of hell in Vietnam during the war there. He earned a Bronze Star and Purple Heart as well. He endured much, as did my Grandpa Ferguson before him, who was a "Dolphin" in the Navy.

I met another Vietnam Veteran while at the Poly-Trauma unit of the Veterans Health Care System in Palo Alto, California. He is the President and Founder of the "Blue Star Riders," a group that visits the wounded in hospitals. He not only helped and looked after me he became a friend a man only gets one of in a lifetime. Thank-You "Wolf," (Marsha too) I love you my brother! You will never realize the impact you have had on the lives of thousands, as you have selflessly taken care of our nations wounded and their families for nearly a decade!

Command Sergeant Major Dell Smith, my dear friend, was always there to check on me; in Iraq, and at hospitals and home, wherever I was, so was he. Thank you my friend! (Connie too!)

To date my journey has covered six major surgeries, at eight different hospitals in three different states, being treated by 47 different health care specialists and professionals. The emergency care has involved again that many, and put ten or more stitches in my face on 51 different times. I am grateful for every one of you!

Thanks to grandparents for countless hours babysitting.

Special thanks to the Following organizations who have helped my entire family and made my recovery and my future have meaning I never would have seen:

The Blue Star Riders ("Wolf," Marsha, Tony and Vicky, Mrs. Hamilton and Big Dan)
Homes for Our Troops (John Gonzales and staff)
The Coalition to Salute America's Heroes
The Montel Williams Show (and Montel Williams)
The Eagle Cane Project (Jack Nitz, you gave me wings)
Wounded Warrior Project
AW2 (Army Wounded Warrior Program)
Vet-Tix (special thanks to Eddie Rausch)
Palo Alto Health Care System, Palo Alto, California (Director Freeman, Scott Skiles, K. Childress and staff; Opthamology: Chief Dr G. Cockerham, K. Glynn-Milley, Megan and Ann; Polytrauma, Bill P. & "Sly")
The Fisher House Foundation (Palo Alto Fisher House and staff. Special thanks to Alan Armstrong)
George E Wahlen Veterans Hospital in SLC, Utah (Dr Gepheart; Dr West; Dr P. Miller; Dr T. Mullin; Poly-Trauma; VISTA, S. Jones; Mrs Karabatsos)
Center for Prosthetics, Inc (Carole and Joe)
Thank a Soldier Foundation (Jared Gomez, God Bless)
Utah Joint Forces Charitable Trust

It is easy to joke and say to friends my world shrunk when I became handicapped. It is hard to accept when I am all alone and a heart and mind want to freely travel and explore a world that I can no longer wander in.

A special "thank you" to some special people who have helped me "wander" along my "Recovery Road:"

George and Melba Wahlen (Medal of Honor Recipient George Wahlen has passed. I thank God for him often)
Jarral Hancock (Wounded Warrior; A giant among men)
My Aunt Marilyn (for endless "pennies" of love)
Toby Keith (Your support of our troops 2nd to NONE)
Montgomery Gentry (your Patriotism rocks)
Richard Paul Evans (for letting me "WALK" with you)
Ernest Chamberlain (Lynn, Grace, Robyn and staff)
Dennis Cattel (Vietnam Veteran, Army Ranger, friend)
John Crosby (CSM[RET], 19th S.F., Army, "All but 9")
Craig Morgan (Retired Colonel, Army, 9/11 Survivor)
Brigadier General Jefferson Burton (Essayons!)
Red Atwood (Get the boat ready)
Scott Campbell (you have never stopped calling)
Kam, Kip, and Ron (you have always been there)
P W Covington (Keep fighting the fight!)
Jim Lish (always has my "six")
Jeff Sagers (Natural Rock Designs, Inc; Dear friend)
Dawn and Paul (great friends at Colonial Flag)
Brett Hutchings(MAJ[RET], Army; Hutch's Furniture)
"Blackie" and Harold (for taking me under your wings)
Jerry Bishop (Vietnam Veteran, "gagon dragon" buddy)
Dave Baker (Vietnam Veteran, my friend and "light")
Matt Cousins (Major, Army; Protector of my family)
Carl Poland and Harold Joseph (your work always at hand!)
Wade Ewell; My "BIG" Brother, My Hero!

A Handshake with former Secretary of Veterans Affairs James Peake (he was the Secretary at the Time).

Resources

The key to gaining access quickly to much needed resources, as well as eliminating as much stress as possible as one navigates the different government bureaucracies and charity organizations relies on two main factors.

First, have you and/or your service member's vital records handy, and readily available. No matter which organization you deal with, or major charity, they will all ask for the same few vital documents, or for the information that comes off of them. You should put together, and have available in one place, at least the following documents:

1. DD Form 214. You may have more than one. The very last is most important. It shows the service members dates of service, Grade and Rank, Awards, Schooling, Total Years of Service and Type of Discharge. You should take a copy to the Department of Veterans Affairs Office near you. They will certify it and keep a file on record, in case you lose yours, you can get a copy from them quickly if you have provided them one.

2. Orders awarding a Purple Heart. Not the pretty certificate to hang on your wall, but the Permanent Order that Authorized and announced the award of the medal.

3. Marriage License, Birth Certificates and Death or Divorce documents if it applies

4. Two Forms of Pictured Identification. You should immediately get registered at you nearest V.A. Hospital or Outpatient clinic. They can direct you where you need to go to get loaded into the system and get you a Veterans ID Card made. Besides being used for VA Services, the card is an excellent second form of Identification.

5. While getting better, the system is not breaking any sound barriers, so to speak. You WILL have periods of long waits, feel like you are in lines that never move, and could get easily frustrated. Three words will drastically cut down on your frustrations. They are patience, Patience, PATIENCE! Best I can tell you, take a book, magazine, or mp3 player with you.

Do not delay getting registered and in the VA system. You may not see urgency now. However, once in the system, you are always in the system. Don't wait until you are in dire straits to get registered, years down the road, when important information is forgotten or documents have been misplaced or lost.

Ask a lot of questions and seek out the help of others who have been there before you. They are willing to help and can save you a lot of time and guess work.

Also, every Service organization has a service officer to assist you in filing a claim or providing information. The Veterans of Foreign Wars, Disabled American Veterans, Military Order of the Purple Heart, American Legion, every one of them have people trained to help you navigate the system.

I would strongly recommend joining a service organization, like the VFW, DAV, or American Legion. Go to an occasional meeting. The people already in the system love to share information, and can pass along, from experience, things to do or avoid doing, which will drastically cut down on your time, by not having to "re-invent the wheel," so to speak.

Remember the Veterans facilities are YOUR facilities. You and only you can make them stronger and better. Do NOT hesitate to tell someone when you do not get the service you deserve. If you find a problem, try to think of a better way of doing things, a solution to your problem. Fill out a suggestion card. They have suggestion card boxes everywhere. It pays to use them! They are not just for Complaints either. If something or someone is doing a GREAT job, let someone know. That way the good things get noticed, reinforced and become common practice, rather than fading away.

You must learn to be the expert. Get current handbooks. Ask questions. Keep asking questions if you do not get satisfying answers. BE PERSISTANT! Remember, they are YOUR Facilities and Benefits. YOU EARNED THEM! Get the most from them. Get the HELP you deserve and earned!

The following is a list of some helpful websites. It is by no means inclusive and there is absolutely NO MEANING to the Order in which they appear. Meaning the first one listed is not better or more efficient than the last. Each has an area of a specific expertise and/ or focus. Each is a Vital and Worthwhile Organization. Anyone worthy of ANY donation you could spare.

All offer tools and information of value, and things constantly change. Check back often.

And Thank-you, by the way, for your service or that of a loved one or friend! Thank you for supporting our Soldiers and Veterans!

Here are the websites:

Homes for Our Troops
http://www.homesforourtroops.org
They are providing specially adapted homes for our severely wounded service members all over the country at no cost to them. They are based in Taunton, MA.

Coalition to Salute America's Heroes
http://www.saluteheroes.org
Helps wounded and disabled military veterans and their families rebuild their lives and homes.

Wounded Warrior Project
http://www.woundedwarriorproject.org
Wounded Warrior Project Provides programs and services to severely injured service members during the time between active duty and transition back to the civilian world. The greatest casualty is being forgotten.

The Army Wounded Warrior Program (AW2)
http://wtc.army.mil
The official U.S. Army program that assists and advocates for severely wounded, ill, and injured Soldiers, Veterans, and their Families, wherever they are located, regardless of military status.

Vet Tix
http://www.vettix.org
The Veteran Tickets Foundation (Vet Tix) gives without prejudice FREE tickets to all Veterans, Active Duty Military and their families. They provide free tickets to every event you could think of across the country, from all Major League Sports, NASCAR, Broadway

Plays and Musicals, the Theater, and Concerts and Comedy; you can make a wish, they will try to fulfill it.

Soldiers' Angels
http://www.soldiersangels.org
Soldiers' Angels is a volunteer-led 501(c)(3) nonprofit with hundreds of thousands of volunteers... providing aid and comfort to the men and women of the U.S. Armed Services. Let no Soldier go unloved.

The Blue Star Riders
http://www.bluestarriders.com
A non-profit 501 (c) (3) charity corporation serving American wounded Soldiers and the families of those which have fallen in the action of serving their country and protecting our American Freedoms, Values and Way of Life. The focus of the Blue Star Riders is on our Hospitalized Soldiers and Veterans, by actually visiting the wounded and providing need and assistance to them and their families in any form they need it. Providing everything from financial support, personal hygiene products, clothing boots... even rides to the grocery store. 100% of every donation goes directly to the wounded and their families.

Eagle Cane Project
http://www.eaglecane.com
Our Goal is to provide presentation canes to Post 9-11 Veterans who have received some manner of leg disability from combat related actions. By the lead of Jack Nitz and the Eastern Oklahoma Woodcarvers Association, Wood Carving clubs across the nation have united in this cause. Each cane a custom made functional work of Master Craftsmanship and Art.

Disabilities Rights Advocates for Technology (DRAFT)
http://www.draft.org
Segs4Vets, Mobilizing America's Heroes. SEGS4VETS has awarded more than 250 Segways to Veterans who were severely wounded.in the War Against Terrorism.

Veterans Administration
http://www.va.gov
Information on EVERYTHING the V.A can provide.

VeteranAid.org
http://www.veteranaid.org
This organization Salutes ALL Veterans; thru Benefit information and how to apply for it. The Aid and Attendance (A&A) Pension provides benefits for veterans and surviving spouses who require the regular attendance of another person.

The following is a **PHONE** contact list of organizations whose primary focus is on crisis and crisis prevention and help programs for ALL Soldiers and their Families.

National Suicide Prevention Lifeline
(800)273-925
note: 9255 spells TALK. (800)-273-TALK.
The ONLY National Suicide Intervention hotline funded by the Federal Government, this number works
24 hours a day, seven days a week and has over 100 crisis centers nationwide. Currently suicide is taking the lives of more of our soldiers than the enemy is in both Iraq and Afghanistan. It has to stop. If you think you know someone in need of help, please do not look away. Help is out there! Help is available!

Military One Source

It is 24 hour help by phone. Help with life's "Big" and "Little" issues. Not a question or topic that cannot be discussed. From Physical and Mental Health concerns, Social concerns, Fear and Anxiety to how to change your car oil or bake a cake. No Kidding! Help is available.
ARMY: 800-464-8107
MARINES: 800-869-0278
NAVY: 800-540-4123
AIR FORCE: 800-707-5784

National Veterans Foundation

(800)777-4443. This is the only nationwide non-governmental national hotline for Veterans and their Families. They provide emotional support, crisis intervention, and benefit information. Also see their web site at http://www.nvf.org

Social Security Office Locator

(800)772-1213. Veterans suffering from PTSD may be able to obtain Social Security Benefits even if the VA refuses them.

REALifelines

They offer Employment Assistance for seriously wounded veterans who otherwise could not return to work. (877)872-5627 (877) US2-JOBS

Less than 2% of the American Population has currently served in a branch of our Armed Services.

No matter what you're political views are...

No matter what your opinion is of war...

Soldiers do not make wars. Nor do they decide when or where to fight one.

What they do, is march when and where they are ordered to, and when there, they do the best job they can possibly do.

This is one reason why the soldier, the American Soldier, is quite possibly the greatest promoter of peace on the planet.

Thank-you, for supporting our Soldiers, Sailors, Airmen and Marines...

Their Families...

... And our "Wounded Warriors."

All Gave Some... and are still giving!

...Some Gave ALL!

G.L. EWELL

The End